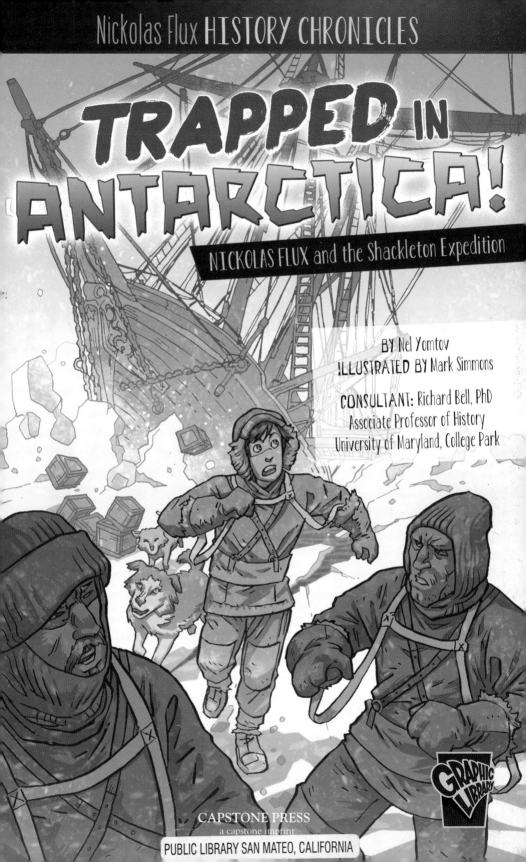

TRAPPED IN ANTARCTICA!

NICKOLAS FLUX and the Shackleton Expedition

BY Nel Yomtov
ILLUSTRATED BY Mark Simmons

CONSULTANT: Richard Bell, PhD
Associate Professor of History
University of Maryland, College Park

CAPSTONE PRESS
a capstone imprint

Graphic Library is published by Capstone Press,
1710 Roe Crest Drive, North Mankato, Minnesota 56003
www.capstonepub.com

Library of Congress Cataloging-in-Publication Data
Yomtov, Nelson.
  Trapped in Antarctica! : Nickolas Flux and the Shackleton expedition / Nel Yomtov.
    pages cm.—(Nickolas Flux history chronicles)
  Summary: "When a spontaneous time leap sends Nickolas Flux back to Ernest
Shackleton's ill-fated Endurance Expedition to Antarctica, what's a teenage history buff
to do? Try to avoid becoming stranded, of course! From the crushing of the Endurance
to a heroic lifeboat journey, Nick must survive one of the most amazing expeditions of
the early 1900s"—Provided by publisher.
  Includes bibliographical references.
  ISBN 978-1-4914-2069-0 (library binding)
  ISBN 978-1-4914-2285-4 (paperback)
  ISBN 978-1-4914-2287-8 (eBook PDF)
1. Shackleton, Ernest Henry, Sir, 1874-1922—Juvenile fiction. 2. Graphic novels.
[1. Graphic novels. 2. Shackleton, Ernest Henry, Sir, 1874-1922—Fiction. 3. Imperial
Trans-Antarctic Expedition (1914-1917)—Fiction. 4. Antarctica—Discovery and
exploration—Fiction. 5. Endurance (Ship)—Fiction. 6. Survival—Fiction. 7.
Stowaways—Fiction. 8. Time travel—Fiction.] I. Title.
  PZ7.7.Y66Tr 2015
  741.5'973—dc23   2014019813

Photo Credits:
Design Elements: Shutterstock (backgrounds)

Editor's note:
Direct quotations, noted in red type, appear on the following pages:
    Pages 9 and 10 from *Endurance: An Epic of Polar Adventure,* by F. A. Worsley (New
      York: W. W. Norton, 1999).
    Pages 13 and 16 from Huntford, R. "Shackleton," (New York: Carroll & Graf, 1998).
    Page 17 from *The Diaries of Frank Hurley, 1912-1941,* by Frank Hurley (New York:
      Anthem Press, 2011).
    Page 25 from *South: The Story Of Shackleton's Last Expedition,*
      1914-17, by Sir Ernest Shackleton (North Pomfret, Vt.: Trafalgar Square Pub., 1992).

EDITOR   DESIGNER
Adrian Vigliano   Ashlee Suker

ART DIRECTOR   PRODUCTION SPECIALIST
Nathan Gassman   Kathy McColley

Printed in the United States of America in Stevens Point, Wisconsin.
092014   008479WZS15

TABLE OF CONTENTS

FLUX FACT

The *Endurance* left England on August 8, 1914.
Aboard the ship was leader Sir Ernest Shackleton,
a crew of 26 men, 1 stowaway, 69 sled dogs, and 1 cat.
Shackleton's goal was to become the first explorer to
cross the continent of Antarctica on foot.

FLUX FACT

Endurance became trapped in pack ice on January 19, 1915. For ten months it drifted with the slowly moving ice across the Weddell Sea—roughly 600 miles (966 kilometers).

I was surprised to learn we had another stowaway on board. How you've stayed hidden this long is beyond me.

But I suppose we're both stuck with each other now!

You've already met your fellow stowaway, Perce Blackborrow. What do you boys have to say for yourselves?

Well, Mr. Shackleton, I was wondering ... how could we have ended up in such a desperate situation?

You haven't told me when you joined our expedition, but ...

... after we left England, we sailed to Argentina. In October of 1914, we headed to a whaling station on South Georgia Island.

There we loaded up on supplies before sailing toward Antarctica. The local whalers told us the pack ice was rougher and more dangerous than usual.

We waited until December and then we finally set sail through the Weddell Sea bound for Antarctica. But luck ran out, and in January we became trapped in the ice.

As you know, we've been here ever since, doing our best to pass the time and keep our spirits up.

FLUX FACT

When 18-year-old stowaway Perce Blackborrow was discovered, Shackleton reportedly flew into a rage to scare the teen. "Do you know that on these expeditions we often get very hungry, and if there is a stowaway available he is the first to be eaten?" he said.

13

FLUX FACT

In his diary, photographer Frank Hurley wrote a farewell to his favorite dog, who was ordered to be killed: "Hail to thee old leader Shakespeare, I shall ever remember thee—fearless, faithful, and diligent."

17

FLUX FACT

The crew of the *Endurance* had spent 170 days drifting on a floe of ice with short supplies of food and inadequate shelter. Before they landed on Elephant Island, they had not set foot on land since December 5, 1914—497 days earlier!

FLUX FACT

Shackleton chose a small crew to accompany him to South Georgia Island including Captain Worsley, carpenter Chippy McNeish, and doctor Tim McCarthy.

FLUX FACT

Captain Worsley used a sextant to navigate the *James Caird*. This instrument measures the angle between the Sun, moon, or a star and the horizon. The angle and the time of day it was measured can be used to determine a ship's position on a nautical chart.

FLUX FACT

After spotting South Georgia Island, a sudden storm gathered and battered the *James Caird*. The crew battled the storm for 9 hours, until it finally passed. "I think most of us had a feeling that the end was very near," wrote Shackleton.

CHAPTER FIVE
A HAIR-RAISING ADVENTURE

The present

I-I'm okay, Dad. I'll be up in second.

I need to look up what happened to Shackleton and his crew!

What?! I can't return now!

Are you alright down there, Nick? You're missing all the fun!

Reaching the whaling station wasn't the end of the story. The next day, Shackleton rode a ship to rescue the men left on the other side of South Georgia Island.

Shackleton tried three times to rescue his crew on Elephant Island. Each time, the ship he sailed became trapped in pack ice and had to return to its port.

The rescue from Elephant Island would be much more difficult.

Months passed. Shackleton had no way of knowing if his men were still alive.

Finally, on August 30, 1916, Shackleton steamed into the waters off Elephant Island in the *Yelcho*, a rescue ship provided by the government of Chile.

The crew's two-year ordeal was finally over.

Shackleton and his men suffered terrible conditions and difficult obstacles.

But they never gave up hope. They conquered everything they faced.

For that reason, after more than 100 years, we still remember their amazing heroism on an unforgettable voyage.

Now how am I going to explain this shaggy hair?

FLUX FILES

THE SHIP

The *Endurance* was built in Norway in 1912 and was originally named *Polaris*. The vessel was intended to be used for tourists to hunt polar bears. It measured 144 feet (44 m) long and 25 feet (7.6 m) wide. After Sir Ernest Shackleton bought the ship, he renamed it *Endurance*, after his family's motto, "By endurance we conquer." The vessel was equipped with three lifeboats: the *James Caird*, the largest; the *Dudley Docker*; and the *Stancomb Wills*, the smallest.

SHACKLETON'S JOURNEYS

Sir Ernest Shackleton's 1914 expedition was his third to Antarctica. He had tried in 1907 and 1909 to reach the South Pole but had failed in each attempt. In 1909, however, he got within 112 miles (180 km) of the South Pole—the closest anyone in history had reached up to that time. For his accomplishment Shackleton was knighted by British King Edward VII.

OTHER EXPLORERS

Despite his persistent attempts Shackleton was beaten to the South Pole by two explorers. In December 1911 Roald Amundsen of Norway became the first person to reach the bottom of the Earth. Weeks later, in January 1912, Englishman Robert Falcon Scott successfully reached the South Pole. On their return voyage Scott and his four fellow explorers died from starvation and extreme cold.

FINAL VOYAGE

The *Endurance* expedition made Shackleton a hero in England. Eager to continue his explorations, he began a new voyage to Antarctica in 1921 aboard the ship *Quest*. Many of the *Endurance* crewmembers signed on to join their former skipper. The *Quest* arrived at South Georgia Island on January 4, 1922. The next morning, Shackleton, who earlier had been diagnosed with a heart condition, suffered a fatal heart attack. He was 42 years old.

CAPTAIN WORSLEY

After the *Endurance* expedition Captain Frank Worsley joined the British Royal Navy Reserve (RNR). During World War I (1914-1918) he commanded a ship that sunk a German submarine, a deed for which he was awarded the Distinguished Service Order. Over the years Worsley kept in contact with Shackleton. In 1921 he joined his former boss as the captain of the *Quest*, the ship used in Shackleton's ill-fated final expedition.

SOUTH
ATLANTIC
OCEAN

MAP OF THE *ENDURANCE* EXPEDITION

SOUTH
GEORGIA
ISLAND

ELEPHANT ISLAND

WEDDELL SEA

- *Endurance* route, sailing
- *Endurance* route, trapped in ice
- Weddell Sea party route to Elephant Island
- Shackleton and rescue party route to South Georgia Island
- Planned route across Antarctica

SOUTH POLE

ANTARCTICA

GLOSSARY

EXPEDITION (ek-spuh-DI-shuhn)—a journey with a goal, such as exploring or searching for something

FLOE (FLOH)—a large sheet of floating ice

ISOLATION (eye-suh-LAY-shun)—the condition of being alone

LANDFALL (LAND-fawl)—the act of arriving on land after being on a boat

LIST (LIST)—to lean to one side

ORDEAL (or-DEEL)—a painful or terrible experience

QUEASY (KWEE-zee)—to be sick to one's stomach, or nauseated

SALVAGE (SAL-vij)—to rescue property from a shipwreck, fire, or other disaster

SALVATION (sal-VAY-shuhn)—something or someone that saves or protects

SCARCE (SKAIRSS)—hard to get or find, or available in quantities too small to meet the demand

READ MORE

BRASCH, NICOLAS. *Ernest Shackleton's Antarctic Expedition.* Sensational True Stories. New York: PowerKids Press, 2013.

HANEL, RACHAEL. *Can You Survive Antarctica?* You Choose: Survival. Mankato, Minn.: Capstone Press, 2012.

JOHNSON, KRISTIN. *The Endurance Expedition.* Essential Events. Edina, Minn.: ABDO Pub. Co., 2011.

INTERNET SITES

FactHound offers a safe, fun way to find Internet sites related to this book. All sites on FactHound have been researched by our staff.

Here's all you do:

Visit *www.facthound.com*

Type in this code: 9781491420690

Super-cool stuff!

Check out projects, games and lots more at
www.capstonekids.com

ABOUT THE AUTHOR

Nel Yomtov is a writer of children's nonfiction books and graphic novels. He specializes in writing about history, country studies, science, and biography. Nel has written frequently for Capstone, including other Nickolas Flux adventures such as *Peril in Pompeii!: Nickolas Flux and the Eruption of Mount Vesuvius*; *Titanic Disaster!: Nickolas Flux and The Sinking of the Great Ship*; and *Tracking an Assassin!: Nickolas Flux and the Assassination of Abraham Lincoln*. Nel lives in the New York City area.